ISBN 978-0-9933626-0-6

Poetry editor: K.S. Littleton

Design: Ivana Kucirkova

Cover: Christina Janoszka

Photographs: Scott James Photography, Northamptonshire

Creative direction: Eleni Cay

First printed October 2015

Eleni Cay

Autumn Dedications

Dedicated to all those who have known the painfully raw experience of losing someone who they deeply loved.

Eleni Cay

A spell-blinding butterfly

Enwrapped in lush green leaves, you did not know
you carry them within, those tiny cells, which one day,
when the time is right, completely dissolve your old self,
leaving nothing behind, not even a little puff of air.

No one quite knows why, but you too
will rupture the hardened case, break the flow of life,
trade a secure base for a few sublime glimpses.

Angel-light, you will forget that you've ever been an animal,
you won't see the autumn leaves bleeding in every Admiral.

Divorce

We sit by our full plates, unsure where to start.

The silence, which used to be a special place
for our intertwined thoughts,
now merely echoes the void in our hearts.

We have reached the edge of our love.
Mascara-tainted tears have etched permanent scars
on the kitchen table.

From now on, everything that life offers
won't make me ripple inside.
The cry of children we never had

makes our story pathetically sad.

Purple

The shelves of your forehead wrinkles
are still undusted. I scrub them clean with hot tears,
carefully placing selected stories
on the continuum between you and me.

I twine our joint years around your neck,
covering you with Wisteria flowers.

In that royal coat I make you believe
there are no blue and red granules
in our blood.

Crimson

I mount fresh buds on the hanging lines,
fragrant roses as though I just came in from the garden.

You dry their lifeblood in the dark,
desperately trying to slow down the decay of petals.

Time has gnawed away our love into a shapeless mass,
lost fragrance crawls the path made of distorted stems.

The well-rehearsed lie that love conquers everything
has become truth, with its thorns,
cutting our youth.

Carmine circles

There is nothing left to discuss.
The rings which used to frame us
rusted into a frayed taste.

In haste, the broken heart packs all our shared nights,
folds them into black bags under your eyes.

Time hasn't washed the scars away,
words we didn't say for however long
hurt in each love song.

At carmine dawn on a quiet lake,
a lonely swan ripples heartache.

Pitaya

He seduced me and I ate.
Ate and ate, till I felt bigger than my past self.

His unrivalled command of language
gave me a high, lascivious fruit
ran down the hair of my peach-coloured thighs.

Cut in half by the possible but never actual,
I succumbed to the licentious rogue:
Mr Potential.

Cardigan

I want to bid an adieu to every single yarn
that runs through the pattern we jointly began.

To all the joint stitches
that afforded us the smooth space
keeping us warm in the far lands.

We never knew that the magic loop
was all about a circle.

Running now in a double row
colourful yarns have become hurtful.

Membranes

Through cold-rolled steel doors
I had built over the years,
a thought of you slipped inside.

Reminded me you still hold the keys,
can come and go as you please,
getting deeper and deeper into my mind.

Till it hurts so much
that I don't notice we are one thing.

Funeral

On the day when you and I died,
aspen leaves sang a D-minor requiem.

Dense woods became a narrow path,
golden sunrays staled into silver.

Broken heart, rest in peace,
we have served your Country of Pain.

The solemn prayer of evergreens
engraved our hurting in a verse,

stirring the sorrow in someone else.

Cindy Lauper, September 15th 1986

We have lived them all-
all the faces of chameleon loves,
the mundane grey, the sublime navy.

But -
tint by tint, our secret tattoos have faded away.

Carefully concocted for love's palette,
our true colours are now flowing in others,

merging into a new blend.

.

Titanic Heart of The Ocean Pendant

A faint fire fragrance dances our romance
to Rasasvada.

Struck by a violin bow
of Chopin's sonata, flickering memories
ignite old aches, heap them into a pyre.

Only a small cry was heard
when you and I became a souvenir.

Reminiscence smoked to blue sapphire the relic of our love.

Thymus serpyllum

Some years ago, we did not know
how to act on love.

Blinded, we succumbed
to the promise of an American Happy End.

Over the years, the deep red of creeping thyme
grew over quartz bedrocks.

Now we just carry on what others have started.

After a quick rise, the rock is broken-hearted.

The ring

Autumn rain weeps into a dark river,
ephemeral drops float in ripples.

Our joint memories wait to be slain
but they are tethered, like wild animals
cornered in the arena of death.

The loss of you did not pierce a hole.
Instead, it burnt a big circle in my soul.

Rehoming

I loved you so much that I let you fly
on the wings of my thoughts.

I made space in the tiny corners
of my mind, so that you could see
the special angle I take when I write.

Without you, my thoughts became homeless.

\-   Until I found poems.

Parting

From the moment you are born,
you start longing for another heart,
similar to the shape you were so close to.

As you grow,
you let go parts of you,
recreating small versions of yourself.

You learn
that deep down, everyone follows
the perennial pattern of love stories.

Children blow away dandelion seeds,
lining in silk the ground for new bodies.

Theology of divorce

When the judge asked why,
We didn't have an answer.

The wish for belonging?
Maybe. The otherness?
Perhaps. The timing?
Most probably.

Between a shared past
and a divorced future,
our break-up granted us
a surreal feeling of presence.

When true love ends,
Religion suddenly makes sense.

Full Circle

We both gave pure gold fragments,
have beaten them out to a shiny portmanteau
covering our joint years.

Its fading echo now disturbs the silence
of our goodbye, inflicts fear upon us,
revenging the ethereal child of our love,
the punishment that we had let out all
our strength in a spurt.

Our memories now exist only
because they hurt.

Double decease

A baby was born.
The mother thanked the Lord.
The father cut the umbilical cord.
All started a new deep bond.

Yet, one day, everything will be forgotten.
Time will dwindle down the edges of pain,

you will pay back the loan,
return everything you've ever owned.

Because to enter the paradise,
you need to lose yourself twice:

you without you
and you without them all.

Lovers in autumn

The scent of cherry blossoms still lingers
on the muddy pavement.

We may never see each other again
or you may become my best friend.

We may pretend that brings less pain.
Either way- losing colour is not the end.

All autumn trees know that.

Marks

What is it that commands Time to bring me again and again
back to our first time in a New York garden,
fresh after rain?

What is it that gives Love the power
to draw everyone in its eternal legend,
to, unpredictably , like the Night Blooming Cereus ,
transform desert into a short-lived magic?

You wrote on my skin songs of longing,
their unfinished lyrics still bleed into my days,
piece by piece shrink my soul, transform the end
into a pulsating space.

Old age

Once shimmering memories greyed into ashes,
witch hazel leaves have dropped,
together with the spidery yellow flowers.

The only thing I hold are a few autumn leaves
spicing up the dull country.

And yet, in the early morning hours,
I can see more than I can feel.

In those moments, God becomes real.

Web

Your thin fingers walk my naked back,
beneath a delicate lace that can sustain morning tears
and summer fragrance.

Tangling my hair into a chrysalis,
Love's insatiable membrane lures in more wishes,
unmercifully wraps them before sucking out all their goodness.

Imprisoned in the sticky threads we make love every night,
nevertheless.

Two seasons

Rivers of bright reds and browns sink into the soil,
sugar maple surrenders to silence.

Winter has little mercy for the colours of life.

But in early spring, buried bulbs rise, ready for the new toil.

The sun forces out a new drop of blood from the inner bark,
desire born out of suffering pulls roots from beneath the mud.

One last walk

We have journeyed all the way to the blackness of birches' skin,
cried so loud that we could not sustain the weight
of our bodies and the tempest within.

We have flown with the wild swans and their wisdom, shrieking
into the sharp memories of labour camps, begging for a new childhood.

We have touched the warm stones of prayers,
re-imagined them into lands of truth,
vast like the haunting melodies of Baleen whales.

We have travelled them all, all the layers of expanding paths
and yet, we long for one more journey, for one last walk,
when we would break apart and in silence grope for each other,
to the deep-rooted you and me, open the circles of desires
and in their gore, swim into history.

Contents

Lightning Source UK Ltd.
Milton Keynes UK
UKOW04n2010151015

260646UK00004B/27/P